ACTIVATE YOUR BUSINESS POTENTIAL

Fast-Track Your Success in Today's Competitive Market

SAMUEL DANIEL

DEDICATION

To everyone who aspires greatness and work diligently to ascend the ladder of success in business; this book is dedicated.

TABLE OF CONTENTS

INTRODUCTION

It is undebatable that today's business landscape is hyper-competitive. However, something differentiates a thriving enterprise from a struggling startup; this elusive quality is the ability to activate the potential in any business enterprise. Beyond survival, how can entrepreneurs prosper their businesses in a competitive market? Understanding the principles and strategies that stimulate successful business enterprises is the answer.

"Activate Your Business Potential" is an excellent guide designed to equip you with the insights, tools, and mental resources necessary to advance your business positively. Whether you're a business veteran, a starter, or one who envisages managing a business, this book offers a comprehensive guide that addresses your unique challenges and aspirations.

Your business can go beyond meeting the market's demands to anticipate and take advantage of new opportunities before your competitors see them. To achieve this, your company must desire innovation, develop a culture that absorbs change, and raise a team that operates at the peak of its capability.

This book recommends strategies for operations optimization, customer engagement, data analytics for informed decision-making, and creating a solid brand. Furthermore, you will learn the relevance of harnessing technology, motivating your team, and developing lasting customer and partner relationships.

Are you ready to transform your vision into an achievable reality? As we uncover the keys to business acceleration, you will be inspired to take every action necessary to elevate your business to new heights.

Let's begin your journey toward business growth, acceleration and potential optimization.

CHAPTER 1

SETTING THE PILLARS FOR SUCCESS

As aspiring business leaders, we are often thrilled by the sparkles of success of "already-made" business tycoons. More often, we need success stories to encourage start-ups. However, you must be careful not to be swayed by the glamour of businesses with towering profit margins. Instead, learning the secrets of their successes is the only proper way to reproduce their results. Unfortunately, several aspiring entrepreneurs overlook this foundational aspect of setting the pillars for sustainable business growth.

This Chapter highlights the vital steps necessary to foster any business' growth and stability. Understanding is required to transform your business from an ideation stage to a productive reality. Moreover, adequate preparation aids in withstanding challenges and coping with changing market trends.

Understanding Your Vision and Mission

Every successful business begins with a clear vision and mission. These two essential elements are necessary to guide your decisions, strategies, and overall direction of your efforts. To craft a compelling vision, you must provide honest answers to the following questions:

- What impact do I want my business to have?

- Who is/are my target audience, and how can I serve them?

- What values are fundamental to my business philosophy?

Once your vision is known, break it into a concise mission statement. Ensure your vision and mission inspire your team and resonate with your customers. This implies that your team and customers must be in mind while crafting your vision and mission statement.

Communicate your vision effectively to stakeholders, partners, and employees. This time, share the vision with individuals who can help you achieve it. It is important to find alignment and enthusiasm within the team you choose to work with. This will happen when you can clearly state your mission statement without mincing words.

Conducting Thorough Market Research

With a vision in hand, the next crucial step is understanding the business terrain you wish to explore. Comprehensive market research will help you discover industry trends, customer behaviour, and competitors. A thorough market research, you should gather data on the following:

- Market size and potential growth

- Changing trends that may affect your industry

- Competitors' strengths and weaknesses

- Customers' preferences and pain points

Ensure you gather qualitative and quantitative data, including surveys, focus groups, and data analytics. The more you understand your market choice, the more you can identify gaps your business can fill, develop meaningful strategies, and reduce the risks of launching a new product or service.

Crafting a Robust Business Strategy

Developing a business strategy becomes easier as you get armed with insights about your market. A robust business strategy details how you will achieve your vision and mission. Essential components of this strategy include:

- **Clear Goals:** Develop measurable short-term and long-term objectives. The SMART (Specific, Measurable, Achievable, Relevant, Time-bound) criteria can help formulate practical goals.

- **Unique Selling Proposition (USP):** Outline what differentiates your package from competitors'. Why should customers choose you? A strong USP is essential for standing out and positioning your brand effectively.

- **Financial Planning:** Create a detailed financial model that includes budgeting, forecasting, and break-even analysis. This financial design helps determine funding needs and manage cash flow, ensuring financial health keeps pace with business growth.

Building a Brand Identity

With a strategy in place, the next step is to build a brand identity that captures the essence of your vision and flows with your target audience's desire. Your brand identity includes:

- **Logo and Visual Elements:** Design logos that evoke the emotions you want your business to be associated with. Be consistent in your visuals or imagery across all platforms.

- **Voice and Messaging:** Establish a tone that reflects your company's character. After developing a friendly, professional, or innovative tone, consistent messaging can help reinforce your brand identity. With consistent messaging, you can quickly build trust with consumers.

- **Online Presence:** A strong online presence is non-negotiable in the digital age. Create an engaging website and leverage social media platforms to connect with your audience. Content marketing can strengthen your brand and attract potential customers, thus building long-term relationships.

Establishing a Strong Operational Framework

Operational efficiency is crucial for driving sustainable growth. Consider the following as you set your operational framework:

- **Team Structure:** Define roles and responsibilities within your organization. Build a team that complements one another's strengths and weaknesses, thus establishing a culture of collaboration and support.

- **Processes and Systems:** Develop efficient processes to facilitate service delivery, customer service, and sales. Technological solutions that automate tasks and provide real-time response can also be implemented.

- **Customer Relationship Management (CRM):** CRM systems maintain, sustain, and analyze customer interactions. This will help you build lasting customer relationships, which are vital for business continuity and referrals.

Embracing Agility and Innovation

The business world is continuously transforming, and so should your approach. Developing agility and innovation enables your business to respond swiftly to market changes.

Within your team, encourage creative thinking, welcome feedback, and create a safe space for experimentation. Having ample information on industry shifts and customer needs lets you strategize as required. With this in place, you have the secret of ensuring growth even in uncertain times.

Creating a Legacy of Growth

Setting the pillars for business growth requires consistent efforts. The six pillars you need to set for achieving success as you aim to actuate your business potential include spelling out your vision, conducting thorough market research, developing a robust strategy, creating a powerful brand, establishing efficient operations, and celebrating innovation. These pillars prepare your business for growth and also create a legacy for the future.

Every significant achievement in business stems from these foundational principles. They fuel your aspirations and gear you towards the horizon of success.

Your business growth shouldn't be limited to physical expansion; it should be sustainable in a way that fulfils its mission, builds its community, and inspires others. Remember that the pillars you raise today will support your future growth—so make them count.

It's not wrong to start small. So, don't be thrown off balance by the solidity of the foundation and pillars you need to set. You need a great framework as a vision to run with. So, don't be afraid to draw a great sketch from the beginning.

CHAPTER 2

STRATEGIC PLANNING FOR BUSINESS GROWTH

Beyond a mere goal, growth is a necessity for survival and prosperity. Static organizations often find themselves behind their competitors and irrelevant to evolving market demands. Strategic planning is essential in guiding businesses toward sustainable growth.

This Chapter explores the essential components of strategic planning for business growth. It provides structures, insights, and actionable schemes that organizations can implement to ensure they thrive in an increasingly competitive marketplace. Undoubtedly, you will succeed if you have a solid plan for success.

Understanding Strategic Planning

Strategic planning refers to defining a business's direction and deciding how to allocate resources efficiently to pursue these goals. It requires assessing the internal and external environments in which a business operates and setting long-term objectives that resonate with its mission and vision.

Strategic planning is crucial for actuating your business' potential for several reasons. First, it clarifies the vision by providing a clear picture of the organisation's future goals. Thus, planning helps align your efforts towards common goals.

Resource optimization is another advantage of strategic planning. When you identify priorities, you can efficiently allocate your resources. A strategic plan guides you in spending your time and money on what matters most.

Third, a well-drafted plan will help you to manage risk. As you consider potential risks and develop plans for eventualities, your business will confidently navigate uncertainties.

Observably, organizations with strategic plans record greater performance in profitability, customer satisfaction, and revenue growth.

How to Crafting an Effective Strategic Plan

1. Define Your Mission and Vision

A well-articulated mission and vision are the foundation of any strategic plan. Your mission statement spells out your organization's purpose, while the vision statement highlights the long-term aspirations. Engaging employees and stakeholders in this process is crucial to ensure that everyone is on the same page and committed to the shared objectives.

2. Conduct a SWOT Analysis

SWOT is an acronym for Strengths, Weaknesses, Opportunities, and Threats. SWOT analysis is a critical tool for understanding the internal dynamics of your business and the external environment. Strengths identification helps leverage what you do best while recognizing weaknesses and highlighting areas that require improvement. Opportunities point to potential avenues for growth, and threats stimulate practical actions to reduce risks.

3. Set SMART Goals

It's time to set goals after clearly understanding where you are now. Use the SMART criteria-Specific, Measurable, Achievable, Relevant, and Time-bound. For example, rather than saying, "We want to grow sales," a SMART goal would be, "We shall increase sales by 20% in the next fiscal year by launching two new product lines." Now you are smarter.

4. Develop Actionable Strategies

After goals are set, the following stage is to develop implementable strategies. These are the particular campaigns and plans that will assist you in reaching your objectives. For example, if increasing brand awareness is one of your objectives, then some practical approaches are influencer relationships, digital marketing campaigns, and attending trade events.

5. Allocate Resources

Strategic planning must include a detailed analysis of resource allocation. Establish the resources—budget, workforce, and technology—necessary to carry out your plans successfully. Ensure that resources align with strategic goals to ensure each effort has the necessary tools.

6. Continuous Monitoring and Evaluation

A strategic plan is a living, breathing document. It is crucial to assess how healthy goals are being met routinely. Create key performance indicators (KPIs) to evaluate the effectiveness of your plans and make any required adjustments. This iterative approach may help organizations stay flexible and adaptable to shifts in the market or internal dynamics.

Engaging the Team

Team involvement is one part of strategic planning that is frequently neglected. Planning with staff members at all levels encourages a sense of accountability and ownership. Organize brainstorming sessions, workshops, and feedback surveys to collect ideas and insights from various views inside the company. Sufficiently, you may incentivize creative thinking and diligent labour to maintain the flow.

The most effective strategic plans promote creativity and embrace adaptability. Markets shift quickly, so companies need to be ready to adjust. Cultivate an innovative culture within your company to encourage experimentation and exchanging new ideas.

Strategic planning for corporate growth is complex and requires careful consideration, a well-defined goal, and teamwork. A strong strategic plan enables firms to endure and grow in a dynamic business world.

Initiating this planning process, motivating your people, and guiding your companies toward a promising future are your duties as company leaders. A strategic plan is your road map to success, regardless of whether you're a startup trying to find your niche or an established business trying to change course.

CHAPTER 3

BUILDING A STRONG BRAND

Creating a strong brand is essential for attracting new business and keeping existing clients loyal. A strong brand sets a company apart in a crowded market. This Chapter examines the key elements of creating a strong brand: identity, consistency, emotional connection, and adaptability. In today's business world, a brand is more than just making a catchy logo or tagline. It embodies a company's values, vision, and customer promise.

Defining Your Brand Identity

A brand identity includes elements like the brand name, logo, colour, typography, and messaging. These elements visually and verbally represent what your brand stands for. To develop a strong brand identity, you should:

1. Understand Your Core Values

Your company's core beliefs should be reflected in your brand identity. Think about your values and what you want people to connect with your brand. Do you prioritize sustainability? Creativity?

Superiority? Clearly define these guiding principles since they will direct all branding initiatives.

2. Recognize Your Viewers

Developing a great brand requires a thorough understanding of your target market. Create thorough buyer personas that include their interests, desires, pain spots, and demographics. This information allows you to customize your messaging and visual identity to appeal to your target demographic.

3. Create a Unique Value Proposition

Your unique value proposition (UVP) helps you stand out among competitors. It explains why clients should choose you over the competition and what makes your goods or services unique. Your branding efforts will only be as clear if your UVP is strong.

Consistency is Key

Once your brand identity is defined, the following step is to ensure consistency across all channels and touchpoints. A consistent brand strengthens its presence and builds trust with consumers. However, to maintain consistency:

1. Develop Brand Guidelines

Create a thorough set of standards for your brand that specify how it should be communicated orally and graphically. Rules pertaining to logos, colour schemes, typography, tone of voice, and messaging should be included. Clear rules will make it easier to keep your brand identity consistent across all platforms and marketing collateral.

2. Train Your Team

Employees should be knowledgeable about your company's standards and values as they are its representatives. Provide training sessions or seminars to ensure that everyone is aware of the brand's identity and knows how to express it successfully in customer support, sales, or social media.

3. Monitor Your Brand Presence

Keep a close eye on how your brand is perceived in the market. Review your marketing materials, social media profiles, and customer interactions regularly. Consistency can fade over time if not effectively managed, so a deliberate approach is necessary.

Foster an Emotional Connection

Human connection and empathy are decisive elements for developing a brand. Strong consumer loyalty is produced by brands that emotionally connect with their audience. To build this connection:

1. Tell Your Story

Every brand has a narrative to share. Telling the story of your brand's beginnings, struggles, and victories can build trust and a strong emotional bond with your audience. Thanks to storytelling, customers will feel more involved in your brand when they can relate to it on a personal level.

2. Engage with Your Audience

Use social media and community involvement to start a conversation with your viewers. Promote remarks, answer questions, and participate in pertinent discussions. By giving your clients a sense of being acknowledged and appreciated, you may increase their emotional bond with your business.

3. Create Meaningful Experiences

Go beyond transactions and concentrate on giving your clients experiences they won't soon forget. Strive to make a lasting impression consistent with your brand values, whether that be via community participation, individualized encounters, or excellent customer service.

Adaptability: Evolving with the Times

Sustaining brand power in a market that is changing quickly requires agility. Brands are more likely to succeed in the long run when they change without losing sight of who they are. To guarantee that your brand is still relevant:

1. Stay Informed

Keep an eye on developments in technology, customer behavior, and industry trends. Being aware of the environment allows you to change course as needed while maintaining the integrity of your brand.

2. Solicit Feedback

Ask your consumers regularly for feedback about your products—both within and outside your brand. By using the insightful information this feedback offers about potential areas for innovation and development, you can modify your branding to better serve your target audience.

3. Embrace Innovation

Don't be scared of the market's dynamic nature. Instead, adopt innovative techniques, marketing plans, and new technology that complement your brand's core principles. Innovation may revitalize your business, whether by exploiting social media trends, investigating e-commerce platforms, or addressing environmental sustainability.

In addition to drawing in new clients, you can build lasting connections with existing ones by clearly establishing your brand identity, staying consistent, creating an emotional connection with your audience, and being flexible in the face of change.

A successful brand is a commitment to your consumers, values, and future vision, not just a commercial tactic. Let your brand be a shining example of what it stands for while the market changes.

CHAPTER 4

MARKETING AND SALES STRATEGIES

Any organization hoping for sustainable growth must have an efficient marketing and sales strategy. Knowing your industry, identifying client demands, and using cutting-edge techniques are essential elements of winning strategies, and they set business owners apart from their competitors.

In this Chapter, we'll examine various sales and marketing tactics that may help organizations grow, the resources needed to implement these tactics, and the significance of matching sales and marketing for maximum effect.

Understanding the Market Landscape

A solid grasp of the market environment is essential before launching any marketing or sales plan. This entails determining the target audiences and learning their habits, tastes, and problems. In-depth market research may include focus groups, questionnaires, and the analysis of current data to create consumer profiles.

You need to understand the nature of your market; customer personas will help you achieve this. The persona is a depiction of your ideal clients derived from actual data and research. They assist companies in identifying their target audience, enabling customized marketing plans. A tech business may create personas with distinct messages and value propositions for early adopters, tech-savvy customers, and budget-conscious shoppers.

Crafting the Marketing Mix

The foundation of any marketing strategy is the classic four Ps: Product, Price, Place, and Promotion. This framework helps marketers develop their offers.

1. Product

Your product must satisfy your target audience's wants and desires. Regular feedback can inspire developments that turn your product into a solution that buyers won't be able to refuse. To ensure your products are still relevant, test them and get input from customers regularly.

2. Price

Pricing strategy has a big impact on what people decide to buy. Approaches like value-based pricing, competitive pricing, and discounting can assist companies in drawing in and keeping clients.

Gaining insight into the psychological components of pricing, including price anchoring, may also be helpful.

3. Place

Distribution networks are essential to your product's accessibility. Given the growth of e-commerce, businesses should consider both online and physical channels. An omnichannel strategy, which integrates all sales channels, guarantees a smooth customer experience.

4. Promotion

Promotion includes all marketing messages aimed at the intended audience. Public relations, content marketing, advertising, and social media participation can all fall under this category. Every channel functions differently. For example, email marketing is superior in B2B communications, while social media is great for connecting with younger people.

Leveraging Digital Marketing

Businesses that use online platforms will have an advantage over their competitors in the digital era. Digital marketing tactics enable focused efforts and yield quantifiable outcomes.

1. Email Marketing

Email marketing is one of the most economical techniques. It enables companies to speak with specific consumers directly. Segmenting your email list and sending messages, promotions, and content to the right audiences can improve engagement and conversion rates.

2. Social Media Marketing

Social media platforms facilitate personal connections between businesses and their audience. A strong social media strategy, whether through interesting posts, stories, or sponsored commercials, may greatly increase brand exposure and loyalty.

3. Search Engine Optimization (SEO)

With so many websites competing for attention, SEO ensures your company appears higher in search engine results. By strategically using pertinent keywords, creating high-quality content, and optimizing your website, you can improve online exposure and draw in organic visitors.

4. Content Marketing

Content marketing aims to provide your audience with valuable, pertinent material. It creates authority in your profession and enables trust. Blogs, videos, eBooks, and infographics can educate potential buyers and eventually help them make a purchase.

Aligning Sales and Marketing

The gap between the marketing and sales departments is a typical mistake many firms make. Effective collaboration between both departments results in higher lead quality and organisation conversion rates.

Regular meetings foster collaboration between the marketing and sales teams. Both teams may modify their approaches as necessary by exchanging information about incoming leads, customer reviews, and sales figures.

To develop a cohesive approach, it is important to comprehend the whole consumer experience, from awareness to consideration to purchase. Marketing may generate leads, and sales can develop them further by offering tailored follow-ups and solutions.

Measuring Success

No plan is complete without measurement. Setting up key performance indicators (KPIs) enables companies to assess the effectiveness of their sales and marketing initiatives. Conversion rates, client acquisition expenses, and customer lifetime value are a few metrics essential for evaluating strategy effectiveness and recommending changes.

A/B Testing

Utilizing A/B testing can improve marketing strategy decision-making. Businesses can enhance performance by comparing two variants of a campaign, such as landing page designs or email subject lines, to see which works better.

A successful firm depends heavily on its marketing and sales techniques for client acquisition, retention, and profitability. Remaining flexible and keeping the consumer in mind will guarantee that your plans are successful and your company grows as the industry changes.

CHAPTER 5

FINANCIAL MANAGEMENT FOR BUSINESS GROWTH

Achieving sustainable growth depends critically on our capacity for efficient financial management. Financial management includes strategic planning, running operations smoothly, and making well-informed decisions that shape a company's future. It is not just about crunching statistics.

I hope you are curious about the financial management concepts that may drive a company's expansion while maintaining stability and adaptability in the face of constantly shifting market conditions.

The Basics

Financial management involves planning, arranging, directing, and managing financial operations related to the acquisition and use of funds. Budgeting, forecasting, cash flow management, investment research, and financial reporting are some of its essential elements. Every component is essential to creating a comprehensive strategy for company expansion.

Strategic financial planning is at the core of financial management. It begins with establishing specific goals aligning with the company's vision. A strategic plan helps firms identify areas that need investment for development by laying the foundation for resource allocation. For example, if a firm wants to grow its market share, the financial plan must set aside money for marketing campaigns, product development, and hiring additional staff.

However, budgeting aids companies in balancing profitability and cost control. It entails devising a strategy for allocating funds while considering operational requirements and budgetary realities.

A well-thought-out budget acts as a growth plan for the company. As a business owner, you can detect differences between expected and actual performance by routinely reviewing the budget, which enables you to take prompt remedial action.

Cash Flow Management and Forecasting

A company's ability to control its cash flow is essential to its continued financial stability. Organizations with positive cash flow are better equipped to finance innovation, pay operating costs, and handle unanticipated obstacles. Strong cash flow allows a business to take advantage of possibilities in new markets, which is crucial for expansion.

By creating cash flow projections, you can better predict your financial demands and handle excess cash. You can also forecast cash inflows and outflows and ensure that you reserve enough liquidity to support growth plans by evaluating historical data and market circumstances.

Investment Analysis: Maximizing Returns

Investment decisions greatly impact business growth. Employing rigorous investment research techniques, such as Payback Period, Internal Rate of Return, and Net Present Value (NPV) computations, guarantees that companies choose projects that best meet their future returns and are in line with their strategic objectives.

Diversification is another effective tactic in the quest for expansion. Financial managers must weigh the benefits and drawbacks of breaking into untapped markets or creating brand-new goods. In a competitive market, a diverse portfolio may reduce risk and open up new opportunities for revenue development.

Financial Reporting: Measuring Performance

Precise financial reporting facilitates well-informed decision-making and offers insights into your business's operation. The balance sheet, income statement, and cash flow statement are examples of key financial statements that provide important details about your business's condition.

Make sure the performance measures you create align with your company's objectives. Success is measured using Key Performance Indicators (KPIs), which include profit margins, return on equity (ROE), and return on assets (ROA) as benchmarks. Frequent examination of these measures enables the discovery of patterns that guide the strategic turns required for long-term expansion.

Risk Management: Protecting Growth

Financial hazards are not uncommon in the business world. They range from market volatility to operational inefficiencies. Therefore, a proactive approach to risk management entails identifying possible dangers and formulating countermeasures.

Companies can withstand challenging economic times by integrating risk management into financial planning. Strategies such as keeping sufficient reserves, diversifying revenue sources, and obtaining the right insurance coverage may strengthen long-term growth prospects may strengthen long-term growth prospects. These actions can act as a buffer against unanticipated obstacles.

Financial management software may improve accuracy, accelerate processes, and give real-time financial performance data. By leveraging technologies like data analytics and cloud computing, organizations may make data-driven choices that fuel expansion.

Furthermore, automating repetitive financial processes like payroll, reconciliation, and invoicing may save time and resources. By increasing operational efficiency, businesses may concentrate more on strategic activities that are essential for growth.

CHAPTER 6

OPERATIONS AND EFFICIENCY

Although every company wants to grow, the key to sustained success is how well it runs. A thorough understanding of operations and efficiency may activate your company's potential for development. This Chapter will examine the key elements of operational efficiency and provide strategic approaches to improving them.

Operations include all procedures and actions that facilitate the provision of goods and services to clients. This covers everything from order fulfilment and customer service to supply chain management, production, and logistics.

Operations are the foundation of your company since they dictate your capacity to satisfy client requests, adapt to shifting market conditions, and eventually increase profitability.

The Significance of Operational Efficiency

The capacity of a company to supply goods or services as cheaply as possible without sacrificing

41

quality standards is known as operational efficiency. When a company runs effectively:

- **Costs are reduced:** By minimizing waste and streamlining processes, you can cut costs significantly.

- **Quality is enhanced:** Efficient operations result in fewer errors and higher quality output, which boosts customer utility.

- **Speed and agility improve:** Effective operations provide quicker turnaround times, which in a market where prompt reaction is essential allows your company to take advantage of possibilities as they present themselves.

- **Scalability is facilitated:** Scaling an effective operational model is more straightforward and prevents chaos from arising from rapid development.

Critical Strategies for Improving Operations and Efficiency

1. **Conduct an Operations Audit**

To improve operational efficiency, you must first evaluate your present procedures. An operations audit assesses each facet of your company's operations to spot redundant tasks, bottlenecks, and potential improvement areas. Collect input from your group, examine performance indicators, and identify areas of inefficiency.

1. **Automation and Technology Integration**

Using technology in your business processes may increase output significantly. Automation solutions may take care of monotonous jobs, giving your employees more time for higher-value work. Project management systems, data analytics tools, and customer relationship management (CRM) should all be considered investments as they may reveal patterns and inefficiencies in your business processes.

2. **Streamlining Processes**

Streamlining operations is the next step after identifying inefficient regions. This might entail establishing standard operating procedures (SOPs), eliminating pointless stages, or streamlining workflows. Seek opportunities to use lean concepts, which support process optimization and waste removal.

3. **Employee Training and Engagement**

Your most valuable asset is your workforce, so training them is an essential investment. Employees with proper training are more productive and may offer suggestions for enhancing operations. Promote a culture of continuous improvement where team members actively contribute to process improvement and feedback is appreciated.

4. Supplier and Partner Collaboration

Good connections with partners and suppliers can improve supply chain efficiency. Work closely with these parties to get better terms, uphold a high-quality standard, and guarantee on-time delivery. Establishing a network of trustworthy partners may help operations run more smoothly and with fewer delays.

5. Utilize Data for Decision-Making

In the information era, making decisions based on facts is crucial. Analyze your operations with analytics to identify areas that need improvement. Using key performance indicators (KPIs), you may monitor efficiency parameters, such as manufacturing timelines, order correctness, and customer feedback. You may use this data to make well-informed decisions that support operational expansion.

6. **Regular Review and Adaptation**

As the business environment evolves, so too should your operational plans. Review your procedures regularly in light of emerging technology, consumer patterns, and market trends. Encourage your staff to adopt an agile attitude so that your company is ready to quickly adjust to possibilities or problems from the outside.

Improving operations and efficiency is a continuous commitment to excellence, not just a chore to cross off your growth strategy. You are responsible for preparing the ground for scalable development and long-term success by streamlining your operational procedures, utilizing technology, and motivating your staff.

Recall that efficient operations may spur development, while inefficient ones limit the potential for corporate expansion. As you learn and apply the art of operational excellence, you will happily see your company grow.

CHAPTER 7

BUILDING A WINNING TEAM

Your staff is the most valuable resource you have as an entrepreneur. A company can only succeed if it has the support of a committed, knowledgeable, and cohesive team working toward the same goal. This Chapter delves into the fundamental elements of creating a winning team—one that produces outcomes and cultivates an atmosphere of innovation, cooperation, and ongoing development.

Understanding the Foundation of a Winning Team

It's important to know what makes a winning team before delving into the nuances of team development. Differentiated skill sets, respect for one another, candid communication, and a clear goal are the hallmarks of a successful team. They encourage each other's professional and personal development while sharing a dedication to the company's objectives. It takes deliberate work to assemble such a team, beginning with hiring and continuing with continuous improvement.

Step 1: Recruitment – Finding the Right Fit

Building a winning team starts with recruitment. It's not only about finding competent applicants for open positions; it's also about finding people who share your business's culture, values, and vision. Think about the following strategies:

- **Define Your Values**: Clearly state your company's key principles. What qualities do you want the members of your team to possess? Candidates who share your goal will be drawn to your clarity.

- **Look for Diverse Skill Sets**: Diversity is about bringing together different ideas and skill sets, not simply about demography. Diverse perspectives and experiences working together are essential for a winning team.

- **Involve the Team**: Current employees might offer insightful feedback on candidates during the hiring process. Engage them in interviews to determine possible personnel's cultural fit and compatibility.

- **Create an Inclusive Environment**: Ensure your hiring procedures are inclusive and accessible. This sincerity will increase the talent pool you can access and help you build a cohesive, vibrant team.

Step 2: Establishing Clear Roles and Responsibilities

Having established your team, the following stage is to clearly identify roles and duties. Ambiguity can cause misunderstandings and disputes, which reduces productivity. To make things clear:

- **Create Job Descriptions**: Provide a detailed description of each position's duties, expectations, and reporting lines. This will help workers comprehend their responsibilities within the larger team environment.

- **Promote Accountability**: Motivate your teammates to assume responsibility for their tasks. Implement mechanisms that promote responsibility, such as project management software and frequent check-ins.

- **Foster Collaboration**: Promote communication amongst various positions. Establish frequent team meetings and brainstorming sessions to keep everyone focused on the same objectives and forward motion.

Step 3: Promoting a Culture of Trust and Respect

A winning team is built on the foundations of respect and trust. Without them, morale drops, and cooperation weakens. The following are some practical methods for creating an atmosphere of trust:

- **Lead by Example**: Set an example of conduct you would like to see in your team as a leader. Admit your errors, be open and honest, and display vulnerability. Others will be inspired to follow suit.

- **Encourage Open Dialogue**: Establish a space where team members may freely express their ideas and worries. Regardless of how shoddily their input is delivered, actively listen to it and consider it when making decisions.

- **Recognize Achievements**: Honor both individual and group accomplishments. Acknowledgement raises spirits and emphasizes how vital each member's efforts are to the team's success.

Step 4: Continuous Learning and Development

Growth is essential for a winning team, personally and as a group. Put into practice these tactics to encourage lifelong learning:

- **Invest in Training Programs**: Give them access to workshops, courses, and resources for professional growth. This investment shows that you are dedicated to their development.

- **Encourage Cross-Training**: Let team members get to know one another's responsibilities. This improves their abilities and fosters empathy and understanding among team members.

- **Solicit Feedback**: Regularly seek input on workflows and procedures. Encourage team members to make suggestions for enhancements to promote an innovative culture.

Step 5: Establishing a Shared Vision

Ultimately, a winning team functions best when a common goal leads it. To present a unified front, coordinate your team's activities with the company's strategic goals:

- **Articulate Your Vision**: The organization's long-term goals and objectives should be communicated clearly. Make sure everyone is aware of how their efforts advance these goals.

- **Involve Team Members in Goal Setting**: Include your staff in establishing goals. If you involve them, they are more likely to feel committed to reaching those objectives.

- **Monitor Progress Together**: Check the team's progress toward objectives regularly. Use this opportunity to commemorate accomplishments and adjust tactics as necessary.

Recruiting, creating job descriptions, trust-building, constant learning, and alignment with a common goal are all integral parts of the continuous process that goes into creating a competitive team. By devoting time and money to these areas, you'll foster an atmosphere where team members may flourish, develop new ideas, and work together to make your company successful.

Recall that building a system that empowers people and encourages enduring cooperation is as important to a winning team as attaining outcomes. As you assemble your group, you will see each team member's personal and professional development as well as the expansion of your company.

CHAPTER 8

CUSTOMER EXPERIENCE

Businesses must first put the client experience in today's competitive market to prosper and expand. A satisfying customer experience increases loyalty and turns happy consumers into brand ambassadors, expanding your reach even further.

Which are the most effective ways to improve the customer experience? How important is it to comprehend the needs of the customer? Furthermore, what are some ways to use technology to facilitate meaningful interactions? This Chapter contains the solutions to these queries.

Understanding Customer Experience

Customer experience refers to every connection a consumer has with your brand—before, during, and after a purchase—is included in the customer experience. It covers every aspect, including using your website, communicating with customer care, and providing after-sale assistance. Comprehending this continuum is critical since it helps you pinpoint areas in which you need to grow.

Key Components of Customer Experience:

a. **Awareness:** The initial way that consumers become aware of your brand.

b. **Consideration:** How they interacted with your sales process and marketing material.

c. **Purchase:** How easily did the purchasing procedure go?

d. **Retention:** The standard of continuous involvement and post-purchase assistance.

e. **Advocacy:** Motivating clients to tell others about your business.

The Importance of Listening to Your Customers

Understanding your customers' requirements and expectations helps you provide an outstanding customer experience. You may learn a great deal about your consumers' tastes by interacting with them on social media, through surveys, and feedback forms. This data can benefit product development, marketing plans, and customer service enhancements.

I've listed a few concrete actions you can take. First, conduct frequent customer satisfaction surveys to measure experience and satisfaction levels. Second, use Net Promoter Scores (NPS) to gauge how loyal and willing your customers are to recommend you. Third, hold focus groups to learn more about your customers' opinions and acquire qualitative information.

Creating a Customer-Centric Culture

Any strategy intended to enhance the customer experience needs to be backed by a corporate culture that values customer happiness. Your staff must receive frequent training, and the leadership must support this.

If you need some strategies to foster a customer-centric experience, you have them here:

- Train employees to prioritize customer interactions and develop soft skills that help them flow with customers.

- Empower your team members to resolve issues promptly without the bureaucracy of managerial approval. This will accelerate resolutions and enhance customer satisfaction.

- Remember to celebrate employees whose customer service is excellent.

Others will be encouraged to emulate them.

Personalization: The Connecting Rod

In a time when information is readily available, consumers want experiences that are tailored to their interests. Customizing messaging, offers, and interactions with the help of customer data can greatly improve the customer experience.

Use customer relationship management (CRM) systems to track customer interactions and preferences and apply personalization as a key to keeping customers.

Second, divide up your email lists into segments so you may deliver campaigns that are relevant to particular groups.

Third, product recommendations should be made based on previous purchases or browsing history to make buying more interesting.

Using technology to create seamless client experiences can be revolutionary. Numerous tools and platforms, like chatbots and CRM software, can improve customer interactions.

You can consider the following technological solutions to enhance customer interactions:

- **Chatbots:** Put AI-powered chatbots on your website to provide round-the-clock customer service and instantaneous answers to frequently asked questions.

- **CRM Tools:** For more efficient customer relationship management and personalized interactions, use CRM software.

- **Social Media:** Interact with consumers on social media sites. Responding to messages and comments in a timely manner can improve your company's image.

Measuring and Monitoring Customer Experience

Monitoring customer experience regularly is essential to determining how effectively your activities work and where changes must be made. Selecting the appropriate key performance indicators (KPIs) can provide information about issues that should be addressed.

I would suggest the following KPIs:

• The CSAT, or customer satisfaction score

• CES (Customer Effort Score)

• Retention Rates

• Average Time to Answer Customer Inquiries

In order to grow in today's digital environment, you must invest in the customer experience. You can build enduring relationships with your customers by comprehending the customer journey, establishing a customer-centric culture, customizing encounters, using technology, and regularly evaluating performance.

Remember that producing goods or providing services continues beyond the point of sale. Every business's foundation is its ability to satisfy customers. When your clients find significant value, your company prospers.

In the upcoming Chapter, we'll examine some powerful marketing techniques to help you further in your quest to provide exceptional customer service.

CHAPTER 9

INNOVATION AND ADAPTATION

The capacity for innovation and adaptation has become advantageous and necessary for survival in today's business world. Businesses that refuse to adapt risk becoming out of style, while those that welcome change can use it to their advantage by leveraging it to spur expansion and stay current.

This Chapter examines the critical roles that creativity and adaptation play in business and provides doable tactics for fostering these qualities inside your company.

The Importance of Innovation

Innovation is the driver of any successful business enterprise. It includes introducing novel concepts, goods, services, or procedures that benefit the company and its clients. New approaches foster a culture of continuous improvement and enhance competitive advantage. There are numerous advantages of innovation for organizations.

1. **Differentiation**: It takes ingenuity to stand out in a crowded market. Companies that

provide distinctive experiences or solutions can attract customers and win their loyalty.

2. **Efficiency**: Innovative techniques can enhance operational efficiency. Adopting new technologies and streamlining processes can lower expenses while increasing output.

3. **Customer Satisfaction**: Businesses may better match their customers' changing requirements and preferences by continuously inventing, which will increase customer satisfaction and encourage repeat business.

4. **Attracting Talent**: Companies known for their innovative practices tend to attract top talent. Employees often seek out organizations that challenge the status quo and encourage creativity.

Fostering a Culture of Innovation

To foster innovation, you must create an environment that rewards risk-taking and creativity in order. The following are some methods for developing an innovative system:

- **Encourage Collaboration**: Give departmental staff members the chance to collaborate on initiatives. Different viewpoints can inspire original thought and creative solutions.

- **Invest in Training**: Give staff members the tools and training they need to be creative thinkers. Consider attending workshops on agile techniques, design thinking, or related topics.

- **Reward Creativity**: Acknowledge and honour staff members who provide creative ideas. This encourages people to think creatively and inspire others to do the same.

- **Embrace Failure**: Promote experimentation while acknowledging that not all ideas will be implemented. Establishing a safe environment for failure can result in important insights and ground-breaking discoveries.

The Need for Adaptation

Innovation drives corporate growth, but adaptation ensures they can deal with change well. Many factors can cause disruptions in the market, such as new developments in technology, changes in consumer behaviour, adjustments to regulations, and swings in the economy. However, your business will prosper if you can easily adjust to these changes. Are you ready to adapt?

Key Aspects of Adaptation

1. **Agility**: The ability to react quickly to changes in the market is referred to as agility. Agile organizations can change their plans, products, or services in reaction to new opportunities or difficulties.

2. **Customer Feedback**: Listening to customers is essential to adapting. By routinely asking for feedback, you can discover areas for improvement and modify your offers.

3. **Market Intelligence**: By keeping up to date with consumer preferences, competition actions, and industry trends, you can predict changes and take proactive measures.

4. **Flexible Strategies**: Developing an adaptable business plan enables your organization to investigate various options and modify them in response to new data or situations.

Companies and firms that prioritize these attributes will not only successfully navigate the complicated dynamics of the modern marketplace but also set themselves up for long-term growth and success.

As you pursue your business goals, you should commit to promoting a creative, flexible, and responsive atmosphere. Innovation and adaptation are continuous processes; you will climb the success ladder as you imbibe them.

CHAPTER 10

SCALING YOUR BUSINESS

Effective business scaling is the difference between thriving and just surviving. Raising revenue requires developing a thorough plan that considers workforce management, customer satisfaction, operational effectiveness, and financial savvy. This Chapter will examine essential techniques and doable actions to help you scale your business successfully.

Fundamentally, scaling a business entails increasing its ability to bring in money while skillfully controlling expenses. It is crucial to understand the difference between scaling and growing. Scaling is primarily about exponential growth without a matching cost rise, whereas growth is a linear increase in resources and revenue.

Evaluating your current operations, market position, and overall company strategy is critical before starting your scaling journey. This reflection can help you decide which areas need work and whether you are prepared to expand.

Key Strategies for Scaling

1. **Streamline Operations**

Efficiency is the bedrock of scaling your business. Examine your organization's operations closely to find places where you may simplify procedures. Automation has a big potential impact here. Repetitive tasks can be automated to save time, reduce mistakes, and free up team members for higher-value work.

Examining financial software, customer relationship management (CRM) systems, and project management tools can all help to improve operational effectiveness.

2. **Focus on Your Unique Value Proposition (UVP)**

Recognize what distinguishes your business from other competitors. Observably, a good UVP encourages client loyalty, which facilitates scaling. Based on market research and consumer feedback, adjust your bundles. Ensure your target audience understands your UVP and finds it appealing in your marketing plan.

3. **Expand Your Market Reach**

One crucial way to help in scalability is to investigate new markets. This could entail expanding your product range, pursuing a new market niche, or reaching out to a different geographic location. To find possible chances, thoroughly investigate the market, but use caution. Ensure your company can service these new markets while maintaining the quality of your products and services.

4. Leverage Technology

Technology greatly aids scalability in the current digital era. Purchasing the appropriate technology may expand your consumer base, increase communication, and boost customer service.

For instance, e-commerce platforms can increase your sales channels, while cloud services facilitate simple access to data and cooperation. Obtain data on technology developments and invest in technologies supporting your ascent objectives.

5. Build a Strong Team

A company is only as good as its employees. Make sure you have the correct people in place as you grow. Strategic hiring should prioritize skills and cultural fit. Investing in staff development can increase loyalty and prepare your team for new challenges as it grows. Establish an atmosphere that rewards creativity, accountability, and teamwork.

6. Establish Clear Financial Models

While scaling, it is critical to comprehend your financial metrics. Use precise financial models to forecast cash flow and profitability as your business expands. Establish KPIs (Key Performance Indicators) and benchmarks to help you assess your progress and make wise financial decisions. This may entail contacting financial consultants or using software solutions built for instantaneous financial analysis.

7. Prioritize Customer Experience

Sustaining a high degree of client happiness can be difficult but is crucial as your firm expands. Concentrate on delivering outstanding client experiences to promote referrals and repeat business. Use feedback loops to learn about your client's requirements and preferences so that you can improve your offerings.

8. Consider Strategic Partnerships

Working together can be a quick and efficient way to grow. By forming partnerships, your business can expand into new markets, pool resources, and improve services. Seek alliances that support your goals and ideals; the correct combination can promote progress on both sides.

9. Monitor and Adapt

Lastly, scaling calls for constant observation and flexibility, which is not a one-time task. Review your performance and strategies regularly. Remain flexible and ready to change course in response to fresh information, client input, and market circumstances. Adopt a mindset that values ongoing development and stimulates creativity and adaptability.

Remember that scaling is beyond increasing your sales; it means building an agile, resilient company that can weather any storm and succeed in the long run.

Above all, never waver from your vision and core principles and remember why you initially launched your business. With resilience and practical strategies, you will grow your organization to unprecedented levels and take advantage of chances you never would have thought of.

CHAPTER 11

NETWORKING AND PARTNERSHIPS

Partnerships and networking have become critical components of growth and success. To achieve success, even a lone proprietorship needs to network and engage in some indirect forms of partnership.

This Chapter examines how strategic partnerships can boost your company's stature, encourage innovation, and reach a wider audience. Whether you are a seasoned business owner or a budding entrepreneur, knowing the importance of partnerships and networking will give you the edge to grow your company to new heights.

Understanding Networking

Networking involves more than merely passing business cards at industrial conferences. It entails establishing deep connections that may result in advantages for both parties. Genuine connections that make both parties feel essential and involved are the hallmarks of successful networking. The following are some main advantages of efficient networking:

1. **Access to Resources**: Through networking, one can have access to priceless resources, including knowledge, financial possibilities, and cutting-edge technologies. Knowing the right individuals can open doors that would otherwise remain closed.

2. **Knowledge Sharing**: Interaction with other industry participants facilitates the exchange of ideas and expertise. This conversation can encourage creativity and fresh ideas for handling problems in your organization.

3. **Visibility and Credibility**: Developing a strong network helps you become more visible in your field, which can enhance your credibility and reputation. Relationships with reputable specialists can improve the perception of your company and draw in additional business.

4. **Support and Advice**: A strong network offers a safeguard. During difficult times, other professionals and entrepreneurs can provide support, direction, and advice based on their own experiences, which can be helpful.

Cultivating Your Network

To effectively develop a network, consider the following strategies:

1. Attend Industry Events

Participating in seminars, workshops, and conferences can provide excellent networking opportunities. Choose events that resonate with your business goals, and come prepared with a plan to engage meaningfully with other attendees.

2. Leverage Social Media

Platforms like LinkedIn, Twitter, and industry-specific forums are powerful tools for networking. You can share valuable content, participate in discussions, and connect with individuals who align with your business interests.

3. Join Professional Organizations

Becoming a member of industry associations or chambers of commerce can broaden your network. These groups often provide access to exclusive events, resources, and a community of like-minded individuals who share your professional aspirations.

4. Follow Up and Nurture Relationships

Building a network takes time and effort. Whether it's an email or a coffee invitation, following up with people you meet is crucial to maintaining these connections. Be genuinely interested in their ideas, extend your help, and stay in touch regularly.

The Power of Partnerships

Your networking efforts can be amplified through partnerships, turning them into strong alliances that advance your company. A partnership is an arrangement that benefits both sides and enables two or more to work together to accomplish shared objectives. The kinds of collaborations you should think about are as follows:

1. Strategic Alliances

These are agreements between companies to work toward shared goals while maintaining their independence. For example, two businesses might collaborate on a marketing campaign that uses each other's advantages to reach a larger audience.

2. Joint Ventures

A joint venture is forming a new company by two or more companies that share resources, risks, and profits. Because it enables partners to pool resources and share risks, this approach can benefit projects requiring large sums of money.

3. Affiliate Partnerships

Working with affiliates can increase businesses' reach through commissions or referral programs. With minimal initial outlay, this performance-based structure may help utilize external networks.

How to Establish Successful Partnerships

To establish fruitful partnerships, consider the following steps:

1. Identify alignment

Seek partners who share your beliefs, objectives, and target markets. A well-matched relationship raises the chances of success and fosters synergy.

2. Clearly Define Objectives

Before starting a collaboration, ensure that everyone is aware of the expectations and goals. This clarity will help prevent miscommunications and lay the groundwork for a fruitful working relationship.

3. Foster Open Communication

Effective communication is crucial for any partnership to thrive. Establish regular check-ins and open lines of dialogue to address concerns, share progress, and brainstorm new ideas.

4. Build Trust and Accountability

The foundation of any successful partnership is trust. Show that you are committed by acting consistently, being accountable, and being transparent. This confidence will foster a more robust partnership.

5. Evaluate and Evolve

Review the partnership's progress regularly in relation to the predetermined goals. Be prepared to modify and grow the collaboration as needed to ensure it adds value for all parties involved.

Partnerships and networking are two additional and crucial factors in business expansion. By cultivating relationships and creating connections that benefit both parties, you can use the network's combined power to seize new possibilities, spur innovation, and obtain a competitive advantage.

As you progress in your career, remember that community and teamwork are essential for sustained success. Accept the power of alliances and the art of networking, and watch as your company grows.

CHAPTER 12

MEASURING SUCCESS

Measuring success is a crucial element to consider when expanding a firm. Since success is a complex idea that differs from one organization to the other, knowing how to measure it is crucial for long-term success.

This Chapter covers several indicators and approaches that you may use to assess your progress and make data-driven decisions instead of relying on gut feelings.

You must first define success for your firm before you can quantify it. For some, success manifests itself as growth in the financial realm, such as increasing profits or revenues. Others may be concerned with market share, brand awareness, or consumer satisfaction. It's critical to explicitly state your unique performance measures.

Key Performance Indicators (KPIs)

Key Performance Indicators are among the best tools for gauging success (KPIs). KPIs are measurable metrics that assist you in assessing how well your company is reaching meaningful goals. The following are some essential KPIs to think about:

1. **Sales Growth**: This KPI measures the sales growth percentage over time. It assists you in determining the efficacy of your revenue production tactics.

2. **Customer Acquisition Cost (CAC)**: Understanding the cost of bringing in a new client is essential. If your customer acquisition cost (CAC) is excessively expensive in relation to the revenue that the customer generates, your marketing and sales techniques may need to be adjusted.

3. **Customer Lifetime Value (CLV)**: This measure forecasts the total amount of money a client will earn over the course of their commercial partnership with you. A high CLV indicates strong client satisfaction and loyalty.

4. **Net Profit Margin**: This figure shows the percentage of revenue left over after all costs are subtracted. A strong profit margin is a sign of effective pricing and operational techniques.

5. **Customer Satisfaction Score (CSAT)**: This KPI evaluates customer happiness using feedback and surveys. Referrals and repeat business are frequently correlated with high customer satisfaction levels.

The Importance of Data Collection

To gauge success, you must set up a reliable method for gathering data. Data collection allows you to monitor performance and yield insightful information that can help steer your organization in the right direction. The following are some methods for gathering data that work:

- **Utilize Analytics Tools**: Establishing a dependable procedure for data collection is essential for determining success. Gathering data allows you to keep an eye on performance and provides valuable information that will assist you in leading your company on the proper path. Some effective techniques for collecting data are as follows:

- **Surveys and Feedback**: Regularly seek input from your staff members and consumers. Surveys can reveal areas for improvement and offer insights into employee engagement and consumer satisfaction.

- **Financial Tracking**: Ensure that your financial records are current and accurate. Review your financial accounts monthly or quarterly to identify patterns and help guide your strategic choices.

Setting Goals and Benchmarks

Once you have defined your success metrics and established a data collection process, setting realistic goals and benchmarks is the next step. The goals should be:

- **Specific**: Clearly define what you want to achieve (e.g., reduce production cost by 15% in the next fiscal year).

- **Measurable**: Ensure that your goals can be quantified through your established KPIs.

- **Achievable**: Set ambitious yet attainable goals based on your current resources and market conditions.

- **Relevant**: Align your goals with your overall business strategy and mission.

- **Time-Bound**: Set a timeline for your goals to create accountability and urgency.

Analyzing Results

Measurement should be a continual process rather than a one-time occurrence. Examine your data regularly to find patterns, achievements, and areas that could use work. Think about the following strategies:

- **Performance Reviews:** Conduct quarterly or monthly performance reviews to evaluate goals' success. If needed, adjust your strategy at this time.

- **A/B testing:** Try out various business concepts or marketing approaches. By experimenting with several techniques, you can find the strategy that connects with your target audience the most.

- **Benchmarking:** Evaluate your company's performance compared to competitors and industry norms. This will assist you in determining your market position and growth opportunities.

As vital as measurement and analysis are, it is equally important to recognize and acknowledge your accomplishments, no matter how minor.

Acknowledging successes can encourage team spirit, uphold corporate culture, and inspire workers to pursue new goals.

Remember that in business, the measured things are managed, so take the time and make the necessary investments to monitor your progress and benefit from well-informed decision-making.

CONCLUSIONS

"Activate Your Business Potential: Fast-Track Your Success in Today's Competitive Market" illuminates the path toward unlocking your entrepreneurial potential. We have examined the key pillars of success, from developing a robust business plan to leveraging digital marketing, embracing innovation, and offering an enriching customer experience. As we conclude this book, it's time to synthesize all that we have learned and launch into what lies ahead for you and your business.

Establishing a profitable business is like navigating a huge ocean. Though your vision serves as a compass, storms are inevitable. The question is whether you will be able to thrive or survive in the face of these changes. Thus, the trip itself is more important than the destination regarding your entrepreneurial odyssey.

Most often, flourishing businesses evolve, whether by utilizing new technologies, making changes based on customer input, or exploring uncharted markets. So, ensure that your vision is not static but ever-dynamic as you gain new insights and as market trends change.

Creating a strong feeling of community and looking for possibilities for collaboration are crucial components of your business growth strategy. Think about the alliances you can build to benefit and advance your organization and the people within your circle. Remember that the most successful businesspeople are not lone wolves. They create environments that encourage reciprocal development.

Collaboration and networking provide access to fresh perspectives and unanticipated possibilities. They enable the sharing of resources, skills, and knowledge, which promotes exponential growth. Your network represents your net worth, so as you go out there, make a commitment to finding and cultivating these relationships.

There is no better time to activate your business potential than NOW. Each step you take should be fueled by a passion for your mission and a belief in your vision. Let it register in your heart that growth is a process. It requires resilience, perseverance, and a willingness to accept success and failure as stepping stones.

As you close this book and start the next phase of your business journey, consider the legacy you want to leave behind. Think about your company's financial performance and the impact you will have on the industry, your employees, and the community in which you live. Your aspirations have the power to transform lives.

This is the time to plan your future moves. What audacious projects will you take on? How are you going to polish and fine-tune your business plans? While crafting your growth strategy plan, aim high but avoid setting unattainable targets.

Finally, keep in mind that growth is about more than numbers; it's also about experience, lessons discovered, and connections made along the way. I urge you to embrace this new phase of your company with enthusiasm and aspiration. Accept the excitement of the pursuit and allow each obstacle to help you advance.

You have the resources and expertise to navigate and conquer the challenges of business growth as you set out on this thrilling journey. Your potential is limitless; the thrill of greatness awaits you.